TALI

C000180755

SON

By Linda Fernley

BRADWELL
BOOKS

Published by Bradwell Books

9 Orgreave Close Sheffield S13 9NP

Email: books@bradwellbooks.co.uk

British Library Cataloguing in Publication Data: a catalogue record for this book is available from the British Library.

1st Edition

ISBN: 9781910551325

Print: Gomer Press, Llandysul, Ceredigion SA44 4JL

Design by: Andrew Caffrey

Typeset by: Mark Titterton

Photograph Credits: Linda Fernley, Creative Commons, others credited individually and where indicated iStock

INTRODUCTION

Somerset is a south-western county in England that borders Gloucestershire to the north, Wiltshire to the east, Dorset to the south-east and Devon to the south-west. It's a rural county of rolling hills such as the Blackdown Hills, Mendip Hills, Quantock Hills and Exmoor National Park, and large flat expanses of land, including the Somerset Levels.

For further factual information on the county's geography or history, or to discover which well-known places you should visit and why, may I politely invite you to head for the enormous amount of excellent tourist guide books and local history volumes – expertly researched and complied by scholars and serious travel writers – which you will surely find in any good library or bookshop.

No, it's not our purpose here to share with you the recognised facts about Somerset. Instead, for these Tales and Trivia books we've delighted in rummaging about to seek out the more peculiar, funny, off-the-wall or lesser known titbits about the county's people, places, objects, customs and history. We hope that these morsels will not only add to your enjoyment of Somerset but will also surprise, entertain, or flabbergast you … or at least give you something to talk about when you next find yourself lost for words!

So from fairy woods to follies, WCs to tsunamis and architectural eccentricities, these pages will show you a Somerset crying out to be explored from a different angle. You don't have to read the book sequentially from beginning to end – just dip in and out as the fancy takes you … and happy reading!

Glastonbury Tor looking over Glastonbury
iStock

PUTTING SOMERSET ON THE MAP

The **first Christmas card** was invented by a Bathonian in 1843. It was customary to write letters to family and friends at Christmas, but Henry Cole – presumably a popular man-about-town – never had time to get all his letters written, so he asked John Callcott Horsley, an artist friend, to design a card for him with a pre-written message inside. The original design showed a festive family scene, and read 'A Merry Christmas and a Happy New Year to you'. It proved a popular idea, and in no time the exchanging of cards at Christmas had become common practice.

First Christmas card – Henry Cole, 1843
Creative Commons

The record for the **most number of people in a hot air balloon** was broken in 1987 by the Somerset Willow Company, a leading manufacturer of wicker baskets. The vessel was an impressive double-decker affair, which took fifty merry passengers sailing over the county.

The **world's first WC** (water closet) was designed in 1589 by Sir John Harington, godson of Queen Elizabeth I, and installed in his house at Kelston, near Bath. In most respects it was similar to the modern-day flush lavatory, with a reservoir of water standing in the bowl to prevent odours from the pipe, and a cistern for holding the water that flushed the contents away and cleaned the bowl. Harington wrote a book about his invention in which he expressed the hope that his 'privie in perfection' would be widely adopted. It could be locked to prevent unauthorised use and needed to be emptied twice a day, although 'once was enough provided it was used by no more than 20 people'. The book, which is full of smutty innuendoes and puns, proved very popular and caused something of a scandal, resulting in Harington being banned from court! However, Queen Elizabeth was obsessive when it came to hygiene and discreetly asked Sir John to install one of his 'Johns' in her palace at Richmond and, to avoid embarrassment, they agreed to refer to the device as her 'throne'!

Somerset is the birthplace of the **game of skittles** – the inspiration for American ten-pin bowling – and there is scarcely a pub to be found in the county that doesn't sport a skittle alley. The Paulton and District Skittle League was formed by miners around 80 years ago at the Red Lion Pub in Paulton, as a light-hearted way to unwind after a hard day's work. They are thought to be the longest running skittles league in the country, and today have 112 teams and 1,500 members of all ages. The Somerset version of the game is played differently than in other parts of the West Country due to its links with the miners: teams of eight are divided into two groups of four, representing the night shift, who would play the first half, and the day shift, who played the second. Natives play with wooden balls and nine wooden pins instead of ten.

Apple cider
iStock

There are around 32 farms in Somerset devoted solely to the making of **cider**. Well-known brands from the county include Blackthorn, made in Shepton Mallet, at the biggest cider mill in Europe, and Thatchers, produced in the village of Sandford since 1904. Over 150 varieties of apple are linked to Somerset, including the most famous cider apple of all, the Kingston Black, which appeared in the county at the beginning of the 18th century. The term 'scrumpy', from which Scrumpy Jack takes its name, refers to a particularly potent kind of cider made in the West Country and comes from a word in the local dialect meaning 'a small, withered apple'.

After the bloody **Monmouth Rebellion**, which took place between May and July 1685, no member of the Royal Family visited Somerset for 300 years. The rebellion broke out after James II became King of England, succeeding his brother Charles II. The new king was a Roman Catholic, and many Protestants opposed his rule. James Scott, 1st Duke of Monmouth and illegitimate son of Charles II, claimed that he was the rightful heir to the throne and led an attempt to overthrow James II.

Monmouth had been popular in the mainly Protestant south-west, and planned to build a following to help him take control of the area, before marching on to London. In exile in Holland at the time, Monmouth landed in the town of Lyme Regis on 11 June with 82 supporters in tow, and gathered another 300 men that day in Lyme. He and his following of artisans and farm workers, armed with pitchforks and other farm tools, fought their way across Somerset, clashing with local militias and army soldiers. They first took the town of Axminster, and went on to recruit many supporters in **Taunton**, where Monmouth was 'crowned' outside the White Hart Inn, before installing himself in Taunton Castle. It was a high point for the rebels, who celebrated their victories with drinking and dancing carrying on long into the night. Monmouth went on to take up residence at Bridgwater Castle, Glastonbury, and Shepton Mallet. However, the rebel forces turned out to be no match for the army and failed to capture the city of Bristol, England's largest and most important city after London.

The rebellion came to an end with the defeat of Monmouth's army at the Battle of

Sedgemoor on 6 July 1685 at the hands of forces led by John Churchill and Louis de Duras, 2nd Earl of Faversham. Monmouth was executed for treason the following week, and many of his supporters were tried during the notorious Bloody Assizes, a series of trials during which over 1,400 rebels were tried and either fined, executed or sent to the West Indies.

Taunton Castle played an important role in the rebellion and its aftermath, and Queen Victoria was allegedly so ashamed by events in the town that when she travelled through Somerset by train, she pulled down the blinds so as not to cast eyes on it. Now home to the Museum of Somerset, Taunton Castle houses an exhibition dedicated to Monmouth's rebels, displaying many artefacts from the battlefield and a letter signed by Faversham on the day the battle was fought.

Wells is the **smallest city in England** and Somerset's only city. It received its status in 1205 upon the building of its stately Gothic cathedral, considered one of the country's finest architectural feats. Wells is home to little more than 10,000 residents. It also provided a large part of the setting for the film Hot Fuzz (2007), starring Simon Pegg as a London policeman investigating sinister happenings in a sleepy town, with The Crown pub playing a key part in the story.

The UK's favourite cheese – and the most popular cheese worldwide – has been produced in the village of **Cheddar** since the 12th century. Before refrigeration, people ingeniously avoided wasting surplus milk by making it into cheese, and discovered that pressing the fresh curd made the cheese last longer. This practice, among others, was perfected in Cheddar, and gave rise to the cheese that takes its name from the village. 'Cheddaring' involves kneading the curd with salt, cutting it into cubes to drain the whey, then stacking and turning it. The cheddar then needs to be kept at a constant temperature, and the caves of Cheddar Gorge, on the edge of the village, conveniently provide the perfect environment for maturing the cheese, a process that can take up to 18 months for the extra-strong varieties.

During the Second World War and for many years after, the majority of the milk produced

Rows of cheddar maturing underground
iStock

in Britain went into making what was known as 'government cheddar' as part of rationing, stopping the production of almost all other cheese in the country.

Though the term 'cheddar cheese' is now widely used and refers to versions produced worldwide, 'West Country Farmhouse Cheddar' has a been assigned with a 'Protected Destination of Origin' and may only be so named if it's made with milk from Somerset, Devon, Dorset or Cornwall. But traditionally, the cheese had to be made within 30 miles of Wells Cathedral to be considered 'proper' cheddar. Only one cheesemaker, the Cheddar Gorge Cheese Co., now remains in the village of Cheddar. Their Cave-Matured Cheddar uses the traditional method, with everything done by hand, and is still matured in the caves as it would have been centuries ago.

The caves at Wookey Hole, on southern edge of the Mendip Hills near Wells, are the site of the **first cave dives in Britain**. Since the 1930s divers have explored the huge network of chambers and in the process have developed improved breathing apparatus and novel diving techniques. So far approximately 4,000 metres (13,000 feet), including 25 chambers, have been explored but the full extent of the cave system is still unknown. In 1927 part of the cave system opened as a show cave, and as a tourist attraction it has been owned by Madame Tussauds and, most recently, the circus owner Gerry Cottle. The cave is also noted for the Witch of Wookey Hole – a roughly human-shaped stalagmite that legend says is a witch turned to stone by a monk from Glastonbury Abbey, whom the witch had cursed in jealousy. The caves have also been used as a location for film and television productions, including *Doctor Who*, *Blake's 7* and *Robin of Sherwood*. On 1 August 2006, CNN reported that Barney, a Doberman Pinscher employed as a security dog at

Wookey Hole, had destroyed some of a valuable collection of teddy bears, including one which had once belonged to Elvis Presley, which was estimated to be worth $75,000. The insurance company insuring the exhibition of stuffed animals had insisted on having guard dog protection!

Legend has it that the coastal area beyond Culbone is where Jesus may have alighted on a trip to Britain with Joseph of Arimathea. This is said to have inspired a passage from William Blake's famous poem, *Milton*, now more commonly known as the anthemic hymn **'Jerusalem'**:

And did those feet in ancient time

Walk upon England's mountains green?

And was the Holy Lamb of God

On England's pleasant pastures seen?

And did the countenance divine

Shine forth upon our clouded hills?

And was Jerusalem builded here

Among these dark satanic mills?

CUSTOMS AND TRADITIONS

On the eve of 1 May in Minehead, West Somerset, citizens take part the ancient ritual of the '**hobby horse**' (or 'Obby Oss' in local speak). Composed of a boat-shaped wooden frame, adorned with ribbons and carried on the shoulders of dancers, the hobby horse makes its way up from the quay through the town, arriving at White Cross early in the morning. Accompanied by drummers and musicians, the horse contends with three rival 'horses' on its journey, cheerfully butting

Hobby horse at Minehead
Creative Commons

bystanders to encourage them to offer donations. Anyone reluctant to give money risks a lashing from the horse's long tail – but its visit is still believed to bring good luck. It's thought that this eccentric performance originated as an attempt to scare away Viking invaders, the route showing how far the unwelcome visitors were chased by the hobby horse. Others claim it commemorates an ancient shipwreck at Minehead.

The **West Country Carnival** that takes place towards the end of the year is an annual highlight in Somerset, and includes some of the biggest illuminated processions in the world. The celebration dates back to 1605 and the Gunpowder Plot, after which Guy Fawkes' failure to blow up Parliament was keenly celebrated by the strongly Protestant towns of the south-west. It began in Bridgwater with the placing of a 'guy' on the bonfire, still widespread practice in England today, but over the years has evolved into dazzling processions of floats, music and dancers occurring all around the county and lasting several months. Around 150,000 people attend every year.

The **Guy Fawkes Carnival** of Bridgwater is the oldest and most spectacular circuit of all, and begins with over a hundred floats decked in lights taking off at Bridgwater on 5 November. The procession goes on to Burnham-on-Sea, North Petherton, Shepton Mallet, Wells, Glastonbury, and finally Weston-super-Mare. After the procession, locals take part in the tradition of 'squibbing', unique to Bridgwater. Around a hundred 'squibbers' stand in line in the High Street, holding up long poles with fireworks or 'squibs' on the end, which are all lit together and make for a magnificent finale.

Wassailing is one of Somerset's oldest traditions, dating back around 1,500 years. Wassail, from the Anglo-Saxon *waes hael*, meaning 'good health', was a drink made from mulled ale, curdled cream, roasted apples, eggs, cloves, ginger, nutmeg and sugar, and traditionally served in large bowls. Around the 1600s, when many Somerset folk worked on cider farms, the wassail came to include a ceremony intended to ensure a plentiful apple harvest. Farm labourers would first perform a 'dominating' ritual, which involved firing guns into the branches to ward off evil spirits. Then came the 'appeasing' ritual to awaken the trees, when cider would be poured on to the roots, and slices of toast soaked in cider stuck onto the branches, to encourage the trees to produce plenty of fruit. An old rhyme accompanying the rituals goes:

Wassaile the trees, that they may beare
You many a Plum and many a Peare;
For more or lesse fruits they will bring,
As you do give them Wassailing.

Wassails are still held every autumn in Carhampton and Dunster, usually around Old Christmas Eve (5 January) or Old Twelfth Night (17 January). Clevedon in North Somerset holds its wassail in the Clevedon Community Orchard, joined by a sizeable crowd and Morris dancers all wishing one another 'waes hael'. The correct response to the toast is 'drinc hael', or 'drink and be healthy'!

The **Bard of Bath** is an annual competition to find the city's greatest poet, singer or storyteller, as part of an arts festival known as an 'eisteddfod'. Local craftsman Rob Miller provides a special ceremonial chair, upon which the victor will sit, clad in blue robes.

Ancient Roman Baths — istock

The Bardic Chair is held for one year, and during this time the city's elected wordsmith will develop artistic projects and lead evening walks around the city. In the Iron Age Celtic tradition, Druids were the law-makers and ceremonial leaders of society, Ovates were mediums, healers and prophets, and Bards were poets, musicians and keepers of history. Each held high status and played an important role in mystical and religious circles. As well as the Bardic Chair, the Ovatian Chair is awarded to a citizen outstanding in the field of healing, ecology or community work, and is held for three years. The Druid Chair is held for seven years.

Wayford Woods in Crewkerne is known far and wide as the **'Fairy Woods'** for the hundreds of tiny doors built into its trees. The 29-acre wood is an extension of Wayford Manor Gardens and was set up as a charitable trust in the 1990s. The first fairy moved in in 2000, when a wooden door with a working handle and hinges was spotted nailed into the base of a tree, swinging back to reveal a tiny bed. Over 200 little doors of all sizes, shapes and colours have since sprung up, along with doll's house furniture and even a fairy playground, complete with miniature swings and slide. Families come from great distances so their children can leave messages, gifts and titbits for the fairies.

But this charming and relatively young tradition came under threat in 2015. The Wayford Woods Charitable Trust became concerned about possible damage to trees, littering from notes blown about by the wind, and 'garish' door decoration clashing with the surrounding greenery. It announced it would take action to curb the 'profusion of elfin construction', which may now be limited to a small area around the ornamental lake – though it looks unlikely that the spritely residents will abandon their homes any time soon!

Glastonbury

Glastonbury is famous for its Tor and for the music festival that attracts thousands of fans from across the world, but did you know that the town is twinned with the Greek island of Patmos, and Lalibela in Ethiopia?

Situated at the foot of Glastonbury Tor is the **Chalice Well**, also known as the 'Red Spring'; this is because of its iron oxide

London Olympics 2012, with model of the Tor — Creative Commons

deposits. Like the hot springs in nearby Bath, the water is reputed to possess healing qualities. The water issues from the spring at a rate of 25,000 gallons a day and has never failed, even during drought.

Wells and springs often feature in mythology as gateways to the spirit world. The overlapping of the inner and outer worlds is represented by the well cover, designed by the church architect and archaeologist Frederick Bligh Bond and presented as a gift after the Great War in 1919. The two interlocking circles are dissected by a spear or a sword, a possible reference to Excalibur, the sword of the legendary King Arthur, who is believed by some to be buried at the nearby Glastonbury Abbey.

In the Chalice Well gardens you will find the Glastonbury Thorn, also known as the Holy Thorn Tree because it blooms every Christmas. The local legend says that this tree took root when Joseph of Arimathea drove his staff into the ground near the well!

'Tor' is an English word referring to a hill; the Celtic name of the Tor was 'Ynys Wydryn', meaning 'Isle of Glass'. At one time the plain around was flooded, creating a peninsula at low tide. The low-lying damp ground can still produce a visual effect that makes the Tor appear to rise out of the mist. This optical phenomenon occurs because rays of light are strongly bent when they pass through air layers of different temperatures.

A model of Glastonbury Tor was incorporated into the opening ceremony of the 2012 Summer Olympics in London. As the athletes entered the stadium, their flags were displayed on the terraces of the model.

The very first **Glastonbury Festivals** weren't anything like they are today; they were a series of cultural events held in summer, from 1914 to 1926. As well as theatre, they also

Pyramid Stage at Glastonbury Festival Creative Commons

involved a summer school and music festival. Because of its strong Arthurian connections, and historic and prehistoric associations, Glastonbury was chosen to host the festivals.

The festival we know today began in 1970, was originally called the Pilton Pop, Blues & Folk Festival, then Glastonbury Fair, Glastonbury CND Festival, and now Glastonbury Festival of Contemporary Performing Arts. It's a five-day festival, which in addition to contemporary music hosts dance, comedy, theatre, circus, cabaret and other arts. It's organised by dairy farmer Michael Eavis (whose full name is Athelstan Joseph Michael Eavis), on his own land at Worthy Farm, between the small villages of Pilton and Pylle.

Festival fun – things you might not know about Glastonbury

- It's the largest open-air music festival in the world.

- Stackridge, a prog rock band from the Bath/Bristol area, were the first ever act in 1970; the event was headlined by Tyrannosaurus Rex – stepping in for The Kinks, who failed to show up!

- 1,500 revellers went to the first festival, where tickets cost £1; numbers expected in 2015 are 170,000, with tickets priced at £225.00.

- In 2014 tickets sold out in one hour and 27 minutes.

- Every five years or so the festival takes a break to give the land, the local population and the organisers a break!

- Amount of water used during the five days: 11 million litres.

- Number of recycling volunteers: 1,300.

- Amount of toilets on site: 5,000.

- Money spent on 'super loos': £600,000!

- The pyramid stage is a 1/10 replica of the Great Pyramid of Giza in Egypt.

- In 2010, the festival's 40th year, Eavis appeared on the main stage with headline artist Stevie Wonder, to sing the chorus of the latter's 'Happy Birthday'.

Floods … and tsunamis!

The Somerset Levels and Moors is a unique flat landscape that extends for about 170,000 acres across parts of the north and centre of Somerset. Thousands of years ago the area was covered by the sea, but today it's a landscape of rivers and wetlands – artificially drained, irrigated and modified to allow productive farming. It's one of the lowest and flattest areas in the country and extremely prone to flooding. In 1919 over one-third of the Levels was submerged by floods and in 2014 16,000 acres were under water. The village of Muchelney was cut off for most of January and nearby Thorney was practically abandoned.

This woodcut from a 1607 pamphlet shows the devastation the water caused

Over the years, many attempts have been made to tame the Levels. The Romans built artificial flood defences to keep out the tides from the nearby Severn Estuary,

Sunset over flooded Somerset Levels — iStock

and dug ditches, creating a network of inland channels to drain large areas of floodplain marsh. During the Middle Ages the monasteries at Glastonbury, Athelney and Muchelney drained and looked after the land, and in the 17th century, Dutch engineers arrived to drain the Levels; ever since, farmers have managed the landscape.

According to some scientists, about 400 years ago a tsunami, described as 'huge and mighty hills of water' advancing at a speed 'faster than a greyhound can run' swept down the Bristol Channel, with the water reaching 14 miles inland and killing 2,000 people.

Arty Bath!

Bath is famous for its spa, the Roman Baths and wonderful Georgian architecture, but did you know that it also has strong associations with the arts?

During the 18th century, world-famous painter Thomas Gainsborough lived and worked in Bath, and John Maggs, a painter best known for his coaching scenes, was born and lived with his artistic family. William Friese-Greene experimented with celluloid and motion pictures in his studio in the 1870s, developing some of the earliest movie camera technology, and is credited as being **the inventor of cinematography**.

'Taking the waters' is described in one of Charles Dickens's novel *The Pickwick Papers*, in which Pickwick's servant, Sam Weller, comments that the water has 'a very strong flavour o' warm flat irons'. If you've tasted it, you'll know exactly what he means! The Royal Crescent is the venue for a chase between two characters from the same novel, Dowler and Winkle.

Moyra Caldecott's novel *The Waters of Sul* is set in Roman Bath in AD 72, and *The Regency Detective*, by David Lassman and Terence James, revolves around the exploits of Jack Swann during the early 1800s. Richard Brinsley Sheridan's play *The Rivals*, a comedy of manners, takes place in the city, as does Roald Dahl's chilling short story, 'The Landlady'. The story tells of a young man, Billy Weaver, who travels to Bath on business. Along the way, he catches sight of a B&B sign and is hypnotically charmed by the sign outside the door and the cosy setting within, so decides to put up there for the night. He's welcomed by a middle-aged, cheerful and talkative landlady, who insists upon sitting and talking with the young man, serving him tea (Dahl refers to the tea tasting of 'bitter almonds', implying that it contains cyanide). Billy is slightly puzzled at the lack of names registered in the guest book, two of which he recalls from newspaper reports of missing men, though she insists they're still with her in rooms upstairs. She also mentions her passion for taxidermy and stuffing her deceased house-pets, a parrot and a dachshund. The story ends with Weaver having drunk the tea, implying he will die of cyanide poisoning, then be stuffed and added to the landlady's collection. So be careful where you stay in Bath!

Bath's famous Georgian crescent – a backdrop for many films and TV productions
iStock

Many **films and television programmes** have used the city's architecture as a backdrop, including the 2004 film of Thackeray's *Vanity Fair, The Duchess* (2008) starring Keira Knightley and Ralph Fiennes, The *Elusive Pimpernel*, a 1950s Powell and Pressburger film, and *The Titfield Thunderbolt* (1953), the first Ealing comedy shot in Technicolor and one of the first colour comedies made in the UK. In 2012, Pulteney Weir was used as a replacement location during post-production of the film adaptation of *Les Misérables*. Stunt shots were filmed in October 2012 after footage acquired during the main filming period was found to have errors!

In August 2003, opera singers the Three Tenors sang at a concert to mark the opening of the Thermae Bath Spa, a new hot water spa in the city centre, but delays to the project meant the spa only opened three years later on 7 August 2006!

In 2008, 104 decorated pigs were displayed around the city in a **public art** event called 'King Bladud's Pigs in Bath'. It celebrated the city, its origins and its artists. Decorated pig sculptures were displayed throughout the summer and were auctioned to raise funds for the Two Tunnels Greenway, a shared use path for walking and cycling in Bath. The route follows the disused railway trackbed of the Somerset and Dorset Joint Railway from East Twerton through the Bath suburb of Oldfield Park to the Devonshire Tunnel. It emerges into Lyncombe Vale before entering the Combe Down Tunnel, and then coming out to cross Tucking Mill Viaduct into Midford. King Bladud is the supposed founder of the city of Bath and is reputed to have discovered the healing powers of its hot spring waters while walking with his swine, which were cured of leprosy when they rolled in the spring.

One of King Bladud's pigs
Creative Commons

FOLLIES

Italian gratitude?

During the Second World War, many Italian prisoners of war were employed on Somerset farms. One night, German bombs fell in grounds belonging to a landowner in West Horrington, badly damaging his walls. Gaetano Celestra, an Italian stonemason, was sent to do the repairs and was given permission to erect a monument as a token of gratitude to local people for having treated the Italians so well. Standing 12 feet high, the statue is probably larger than the local worthy was expecting! It balances on four scaly pillars and represents the Roman statue of Romulus and Remus suckling on their wolf foster mother. Apparently the locals were so 'friendly' towards the Italian PoWs that there is now a sizeable contingent of Italians around Wells; it's rumoured that they may be descendants of Celestra, as many of them are builders!

Romulus and Remus monument
Creative Commons

Jack the Treacle Eater!

Treacle Eater folly
at Barwick
Creative Commons

At Barwick Park, near Yeovil in south Somerset, you will find four follies about which little is known. The official dictionary definition of a folly is 'a costly ornamental building with no practical purpose'. Local wisdom has it that they were built in order to give unemployed estate workers something to do during the severe depression of the 1820s, but two of the follies appear in a painting of 1780, and as they mark the boundaries of the estate at the four points of the compass, it can be assumed that they were probably all built at roughly the same time.

Treacle Eater Clog
Morris Dancers
Image courtesy
treacleaterclog.org.uk

To the north is the 50ft 'Fish Tower', so called because at one time its cylindrical top was mounted by a weather vane in the shape of a fish; to the south is the 'Needle', which is

bent at the top; to the west is the 75-feet-tall slender cone-shaped 'Rose Tower'; and last and most interesting is the 'Treacle Eater' to the east. The most ornate of the follies, it consists of an arch surmounted by a central tower, on top of which is a figure of Hermes – messenger of the gods in Greek mythology. This is said to represent Jack, a 'runner' who during the 1770s took messages to and from London for the Messiter family, owners of the estate. Renowned for his athletic prowess, Jack is rumoured to have sustained himself on his journeys by eating black treacle!

The towers were bought by South Somerset District Council for just £5 when the estate was sold in the early 1990s. A renowned Morris dancing team from Yeovil call themselves the Treacle Eater Clog after the folly, and their costumes of red, black and gold are inspired by a famous brand of treacle!

The Christian faith was a powerful force in medieval Somerset. Parish churches filled the landscape and were often buildings of great architectural quality. Somerset is famous for its church towers. Many of the finest towers were built in the period from 1450 to 1540, not least from wealth created by the cloth trade. This **leather model of St**

James's tower was made by an apprentice saddler, William Weston of Taunton, in 1855. The model can be seen in the 'Making Somerset' gallery in the Museum of Somerset and is part of the collection of Somerset Archaeological and Natural History Society.

St James' Tower ...
in leather!
Museum of Somerset

England's last battle

A mural depicting the very last battle in England can be found on display at, of all places, Sedgemoor motorway services on the north carriageway of the M5 motorway! The Battle of Sedgemoor was fought at Westonzoyland on 6 July 1685, near the Bussex area to the north of the village. It was the final battle of the Monmouth Rebellion (see p8) and followed a series of skirmishes around south-west England between the forces of James Scott, 1st Duke of Monmouth and the crown he was trying to take. The Royalist forces won and about 500 troops were captured.

Also at Westonzoyland is Somerset's **earliest steam-powered pumping station**, built in 1830. Once a guardian of the Somerset Levels, it's now a small museum displaying steam engines and

Steam pumping engine
Creative Commons

exhibits of land drainage history. Pride of place goes to the station's pumping engine, the Easton & Amos built in 1861 to replace an earlier engine that had been carrying out pumping work since 1831.

Europe's first travel book

After leaving university in 1596, Tom Coryate
– a vicar's son from Odcombe – became a
court comic to King James I. James's son,
Prince Henry, took a liking to Tom and when
he left home to set up his own court, took
Tom with him. Tom's father died and left him
some money and in 1608 Tom went travelling.
He visited France, Italy, Germany and others,
covering almost 2,000 miles on foot. When he
returned he wrote *Coryat's Crudities*, the first
ever guidebook for European travel.

Title page of
Coryat's Crudities
Creative Commons

Having trouble finding a publisher, he approached well-known people to write, in rhyme, the introduction of his book, and no fewer than 66 people agreed. The famous playwright Ben Jonson then edited the verses, which amounted to 108 pages of the total 800! Prince Henry then added his influence and a bookseller was found, the book was printed in 1611, and it sold well. Only two perfect copies remain, one of which can be found in Taunton's Local History Library.

Among other things, the book introduced the use of the table fork and parasols to England and, in its support of continental travel, helped introduce the idea of the 'Grand Tour' that became popular later in the century. It also represents a contemporary account of the music of Giovanni Gabrieli and is most likely the earliest English rendering of the legend of William Tell.

Tom went travelling again in 1612, this time to the Middle East and India. Unfortunately, he didn't return to write another book as he tragically died of dysentery in Surat in 1617 although some of his letters home were published after his death.

Ancient road

Considered by many archaeologists to be one of the oldest engineered roads discovered anywhere in the world (and named after the peat-cutter Ray Sweet, who found it in 1970), the **Sweet Track** is an ancient causeway, built with wooden planks, in the Somerset Levels. The Sweet Track extended across marsh between what was then an island at Westhay and a ridge of high ground at Shapwick, a distance of almost 2,000 metres, or more than 2,000 yards. It forms part of a network that once crossed the Somerset Levels. Wooden poles were driven into the waterlogged soil to support a walkway that consisted mainly of planks of oak, laid end-to-end, supported by cross poles of alder and hazel. It's believed that the track was only used for around ten years and then abandoned, probably due to rising water levels. After its discovery most of the track has been left in its original location, with conservation measures taken to maintain the wood in its damp condition. Some of the track is stored at the British Museum and a reconstruction of a section was built at the Peat Moors Centre near Glastonbury.

The 'original' Frankenstein?

Andrew Crosse (1784–1855), a local magistrate, wealthy landowner and pioneer of electricity in the early 19th century, lived (and died) in Fyne Court in Broomfield. He mastered Ancient Greek by the age of eight, and at age twelve persuaded one of his teachers to let him attend a series of lectures on the natural sciences, the second of which was on the subject of electricity. This led to his lifelong interest in the subject. He started experimenting with electricity during the sixth form, after which he studied

Boris Karloff as Frankenstein
Creative Commons

Insect formed
under Crosse's
experiment
Creative Commons

at Brasenose College, Oxford. When he inherited the family estate and fortune at 21, he set up his own laboratory.

Along with Sir Humphry Davy (who visited Fyne Court in 1827), Crosse was one of the first to develop large voltaic batteries – one of which consisted of 50 jars containing 73 square feet (6.8 square metres) of coated surface – which could charge and discharge 20 times a minute, with a noise as 'loud as a cannon'. Locals referred to him as the 'Wizard of Broomfield' and the 'Thunder and Lightning Man' on account of his dramatic experiments.

He was conducting an electrocrystallisation experiment when he saw what he described as 'the perfect insect, standing erect on a few bristles which formed its tail'. More creatures appeared and two days later they began moving their legs. Over the next few weeks hundreds more appeared. They crawled around the table and hid themselves wherever they could find shelter. Puzzled, Crosse mentioned the incident to a couple of friends and sent the results to the London Electrical Society. Newspapers across the country and in Europe picked up the story and some readers apparently gained the impression that Crosse had somehow 'created' the insects, or at least claimed to have done so. He received angry letters accusing him of blasphemy and trying to take God's place as a creator. Other scientists tried to repeat the experiment. One took great measures to assure a sealed environment by placing his experiment inside a bell jar, and obtained the same results as Crosse, but because of the controversy that Crosse's experiment had sparked his work was never published.

Crosse did not claim he'd created the insects. He assumed there were insect eggs embedded in his samples. Later commentators agreed that the insects were probably cheese mites or dust mites that had contaminated Crosse's instruments. It's been suggested that the first seeds of the Frankenstein story grew form a visit that Percy and Mary Shelley made to one of Crosse's lectures in London.

Beware the Beast!

The Beast of Exmoor is reported to roam the wilds of Exmoor in Devon and Somerset and there have been a number reports of eyewitness sightings, but it has been referred to as the 'the famous-yet-elusive Beast of

Exmoor' by the BBC. Sightings were first reported in the 1970s, although it attracted wider attention in 1983, when a South Molton farmer claimed that over a period of three months he'd lost over 100 sheep, all of them reportedly killed by brutal injuries to the throat. The 'beast' has been variously described as black, tan or dark grey. It has been suggested that it might possibly be a cougar or black leopard released sometime in the 1960s or 1970s after a law was passed that made it illegal for them to be kept in captivity other than in zoos. However, cougar and leopard life spans are roughly 12 to 15 years, so this is an unlikely explanation. In 2006, the British Big Cats Society reported that a skull found by a farmer in Devon was that of a puma; however, the Department for Environment, Food and Rural Affairs said that, based on the evidence, it does not believe that there are big cats living in the wild in England. So what could it be, I wonder!

Stepping out – the Shoe Museum, Street

The Shoe Museum in Street is home to Gracie Fields' first pair of clogs. Gracie, a well-known entertainer whose career spanned 50 years, had a remarkable singing voice and could have had an operatic career but preferred the theatre. She was born in Rochdale in 1898 and left her job in a cotton mill aged 17 to join a touring company. She made her first film in 1931, *Sally in Our Alley*, and by the mid-thirties was the world's highest paid movie star. She received a CBE in 1979. Her first clogs, made by a Rochdale clogger, were presented to the museum after her death.

Copy of Princess Diana's wedding slippers
Creative Commons

The earliest shoe on display in the museum is a second-century girls' sandal sole and there are Roman shoes which were found locally near Langport. A selection of footwear from around the world includes an Emir's slipper from Nigeria, a Chinese shoe for a bound foot, kub-kobs worn in Turkish baths and Finnish shoes made from birch bark.

Other highlights of the museum include the 'last' made for Princess Diana's wedding slipper, a replica of the shoes worn by the Queen when she married Prince Philip, shoes designed by Joanna Lumley, Tracey Emin and Terry de Havilland, and a 1923 Perugia ladies' gold, black and silver bar shoe.

The oldest dovecote in England?

Dovecote at
Blackford Farm
Creative Commons

The dovecote at Blackford Farm in Selworthy dates from the 11th century and is thought to be the oldest in England. The stone walls are four feet (over a metre) thick and hold 300 nesting holes for pigeons. Pigeons and doves were an important food source, historically kept for their eggs as well as flesh. The lowest boxes are about 2 feet 6 inches (0.76 m) above the earth floor, which kept them above the damp and away from brown rats, which were common in the area in the 18th century. The Normans introduced dovecotes after the Conquest; the design then was circular with a conical roof containing a hole through which the birds could enter (the Blackford structure now has glass over its roof to keep the inside dry because it's used as a farm store). Later designs included square and octagonal shapes.

Dovecotes provided a means for the owners (always wealthy) to ensure a fresh supply of meat during the winter months. Farmers disliked them because the birds would eat their crops, but it was an offence for anyone other than the owner to kill them. Pigeon theft was a serious offence, and if caught three times committing the crime the thief could face the death penalty – usually by hanging! This example in Selworthy is now a Grade II listed building, owned by the National Trust.

SOMERSET 'NAMES'

Monty Python's **John Cleese** is a Somerset lad, born in Weston-super-Mare in 1939. The family name was originally Cheese, but John's father Reginald changed it when he joined the army in 1915, fearing his unusual surname would make him the butt of jokes. (Incidentally, the family lived just 10 miles away from Cheddar!) In his youth, John was an avid supporter of Bristol City Football Club and Somerset County Cricket Club. As a student at St Peter's Preparatory School, he made his first known comedy gesture, defacing the grounds by painting footprints to suggest that the statue of Field Marshal Earl Haig had popped down off his plinth to go to the loo. Cleese later returned to his prep school to teach Science, English, History and Latin before going on to study at Cambridge and find fame as part of the well-known Footlights theatrical club.

In 2004, John paid homage to his hometown in the form of a graphic novel, *Superman: True Brit*, which tells an alternative tale of the superhero's origins. Clark Kent's spaceship crashes not in Smallville, Kansas, but in Weston-super-Mare, where he is renamed

Colin, brought up to be stereotypically English, and works for a British tabloid, the Daily Smear. Cleese returned to the West Country from the USA in 2010, and now lives with his family in Bath on the Royal Crescent.

J.R.R. Tolkien (1892–1973) drew inspiration from Somerset's rugged landscape when dreaming up his fantasy land of Middle Earth. The English novelist spent his honeymoon in the elegant seaside town of Clevedon, North Somerset in 1916. The trip included a visit to Cheddar Gorge, whose majestic crags made such an impression on Tolkien that they would later re-emerge in his famous *Lord of the Rings trilogy* as Helm's Deep and the Glittering Caves: 'a green coomb, a great bay in the mountains, out of which a gorge

Opening to a cave in Cheddar Gorge
iStock

opened in the hills. 'The steep cliffs became the setting for the epic Battle of the Hornburg in the second book in the series, *The Two Towers* (1954). Heroes Aragorn the Ranger, Legolas the Elf, and Gimli the Dwarf arrive at Helm's Deep as storm clouds are gathering and the siege is just beginning. Gimli is especially fond of the valley's rock, and returns later in the series to form a dwarf colony in the Glittering Caves. On revisiting the Gorge decades after his honeymoon, Tolkien wrote wistfully that the caves were 'still coloured by my memory of them much earlier, before they became so commercialised'.

The great English poets and founders of the Romantic Movement, **Samuel Taylor Coleridge** (1772–1834) and **William Wordsworth** (1770–1850), wrote much of their best-known verse while living in the Quantock Hills, between Taunton and Bridgewater. A West Country boy, born in Devon, Coleridge settled in Nether Stowey in the Sedgemoor district of Somerset in 1797. It was here, between gardening and tending to the pigs and chickens, that he wrote his celebrated *Kubla Khan* (1797) and *The Rime of the Ancient Mariner* (1798). Wordsworth soon joined him in Somerset, and came to stay for a year in Alfoxton House, overlooking the Bristol Channel. The two poets would travel several miles to see one another most days, and take long, contemplative walks across steep valleys, along coastal paths, and through sun-dappled glens. These rambles no doubt provided some of the inspiration for their co-authored work, the *Lyrical Ballads* (1798), a cornerstone of English literature that celebrates the natural beauty of the countryside and a simple, rural way of life.

Samuel Taylor Coleridge is thought to have effectively invented the pastime of hillwalking. It has been said that he could walk the 40 miles to Bristol in a day to attend a meeting, and once walked from Stowey to Lynton across Exmoor and back in a mere two days. Visitors to the area often walk in his footsteps along the 'Coleridge Way', a 51-mile (82km) route between Wordsworth's Alfoxton residence and Coleridge's cottage in Stowey, crossing the Quantocks and Exmoor.

Somerset has a wealth of literary links, in fact. Novelist **Evelyn Waugh** (1903–66), author of *Brideshead Revisited*, lived out his last days in Combe Florey and is buried in the village churchyard of St Peter and St Paul.

The ashes of American-born poet **T.S. Eliot** (1888–1965) are buried in the village churchyard in East Coker. Eliot, born in St Louis, Missouri, came to study at Oxford for a year in 1911 and decided to stay in England, becoming naturalised in 1927. He was able to trace his roots to East Coker, where his family had lived for many years until leatherworker Andrew Eliot sailed to New England in the mid-17th century. Andrew settled in Salem and was on the jury for the infamous witch trials. Now there's a permanent Eliot presence in the village underneath a memorial tablet that says 'Remember T.S. Eliot, Poet'. Eliot visited the village in 1937, and immortalised it in the second poem in his *Four Quartets*, published in the 1940s.

In my beginning is my end. Now the light falls
Across the open field, leaving the deep lane
Shuttered with branches, dark in the afternoon,
Where you lean against a bank while a van passes,
And the deep lane insists on the direction
Into the village, in the electric heat
Hypnotized. In a warm haze the sultry light
Is absorbed, not reflected, by grey stone.
The dahlias sleep in the empty silence.
Wait for the early owl.

Extract from 'East Coker', one of the *Four Quartets*

Also lying in the church is **William Dampier** (1651–1715), who circumnavigated the globe three times and was the first Englishman ever to set foot in Australia. Dampier was aboard the pirate ship *Cygnet* in 1688 when it beached on the Australian coast. While the ship was being repaired he made detailed notes on the local fauna. Because he was interested in natural history he often joined the crew of pirate ships or cargo vessels as a means of getting to faraway places in the hope of discovering new species. The observations made by Dampier influenced Charles Darwin's *The Origin of Species*, and stories of his travels provided inspiration for Jonathan Swift's *Gulliver's Travels*.

Jane Austen (1775–1817) lived in Bath from 1801 with her father, mother and sister Cassandra, where the family resided at four different addresses until 1806. Two of her novels, *Northanger Abbey* and *Persuasion*, are set in the city and describe taking the waters, social life and music recitals there. However, she never really liked the city, and later wrote to Cassandra, 'It will be two years tomorrow since we left Bath for Clifton, with what happy feelings of escape.' Bath has not taken her criticism to heart and the city has honoured her name with the Jane Austen Centre and a city walk.

Engraving of Dampier's ship caught in a storm

In 1964, at the height of **Beatlemania**, the Fab Four arrived at Minehead station to the delight of flocks of young fans, who bunked off school for the afternoon to run alongside their carriage as it pulled in. The group were filming part of their road movie *A Hard*

Day's Night on the West Somerset Railway, beginning on a train to Minehead. John, Paul, George and Ringo were in town for two days for filming, having already appeared in Somerset several times – performing at Taunton's Gaumont Cinema in 1963 and at the Pavilion in Bath a few months later. And in 1967, on their Magical Mystery Tour, they even turned up in Smedley's fish and chip shop in Roman Road (now the Phoenix Chinese Takeaway) to enjoy a traditional British dinner alongside the locals!

Everybody's favourite 'Scrumpy and Western' band **The Wurzels** hail from Somerset. Frontman Alan John 'Adge' Cutler, born in Portishead in 1930 and known as 'the Bard of Avonmouth', is widely hailed as the father of the genre. Adge's years spent working odd jobs around the county – including a stint in a cider mill, naturally – formed the basis for much of the group's material, which celebrates the ups and downs of rural life in Somerset. As well as being sung in the distinctive Somerset accent, the Wurzels' songs are shining examples of dry West Country humour, including such hits as 'Somerset Born and Proud', 'I Am a Cider Drinker' and of course, the 1976 Number One 'Combine Harvester'.

The real-life hill that **Jack and Jill** fell down in the much-loved nursery rhyme can be found in the village of Kilmersdon. Schoolchildren still climb the steep footpath every morning to attend the primary school at the top, passing marker stones along the way that each bear a line of the poem. The rhyme is thought to come from a time when King Charles I tried to reform taxes on alcohol. He was blocked by Parliament, so ruled that the volume of a 'jack' – or half a pint – be reduced, while the tax stayed the same, inspiring the line 'Jack fell down and broke his crown'. A quarter pint, or 'gill', also became smaller after his ruling – thus 'Jill came tumbling after'.

But an even older, more romantic story, stated on the side of the school, says that Jack and Jill were a young couple from Kilmersdon, who were expecting a baby. As Jack was climbing the hill to fetch water from the well one day, a boulder broke away from the nearby Badstone Quarry and crushed him. Sadly, Jill died not long after her sweetheart, just as she had given birth

Kilmersdon — the village of Jack and Jill fame

to a son. However, the boy was in good hands with the villagers, who raised him as their own. They referred to him as 'Jill's son', supposedly giving rise to the first 'Gilson', still a common surname in the area today.

Conservative politician and writer **Benjamin Disraeli** (1804–81) unsuccessfully stood for election as the MP for Taunton in 1835. Many of his early political appearances took place on what is now the 1st XI cricket pitch of King's College, Taunton. The Irish MP Daniel O'Connell, mistakenly believing Disraeli had slandered him in the run-up to the election, called him 'a reptile … just fit now, after being twice discarded by the people, to become a Conservative'. However, despite these defeats and the verbal pummellings, Disraeli proved himself more than worthy of the people's respect, going on to serve two terms as Prime Minister. He made it clear that there were no hard feelings in his letter 'To the Electors and Inhabitants of the Borough of Taunton': 'Whatever may be the fate of my political struggles in your Borough, I can never forget the kindness and hospitality which I have experienced under your roofs; I must always feel that as a body, whatever may be your opinions, you are entitled to and possess my respect; and that for many of your members individually, I entertain a sincere regard and affection.'

Haile Selassie I (1892–1975), the last Emperor of Ethiopia, fled in with his family to Bath in 1936 after the Italian invasion of his country. Over the next five years spent in exile, he stayed mainly at Bath's Fairfield House, devoting his time to writing his autobiography and taking morning strolls around the grand old Georgian House. Several of his children were educated at King's College in Taunton, and the Emperor presented the awards there at the end of each academic year. On his return to Ethiopia in 1941, reinstated with support from Britain, he donated Fairfield House to the city of Bath as a care home. Today it's used as a meeting centre by the city's various community groups.

Born with the name Ras Tafari, Selassie is also the messiah of the Rastafari movement that began in Jamaica in the 1930s. Jamaicans believe his coronation in 1930 was the fulfilment of a prophecy, and devotees still travel to Bath to celebrate the anniversary of his coronation at Rastafarian-led events open to everybody.

MISCELLANEOUS

Little-known Somerset hero **Frank Edward Foley** was born in the market town of Highbridge in 1884. As a top spy in Berlin during the Second World War, he's believed to have saved the lives of around 10,000 German Jews, risking his own life and freedom in the process. Frank used his role in the Passport Office as a cover for his true job as an Intelligence Officer for the British Secret Service (later MI6). In the years after Hitler came to power, without the protection of diplomatic immunity, he entered

Frank Edward Foley Memorial, Highbridge
nr Burnham-on-Sea (sculptor Jonathan Sells)
Creative Commons

concentration camps to present visas allowing prisoners to be freed to travel, hid Jews in his home, and used his skills and knowledge to help them obtain false papers and passports.

His repeated acts of kindness and bravery went unsung in his own lifetime, but in 1999 he was recognised as 'Righteous Among the Nations' in Israel, and on 24 November 2004, on what would have been his 120th birthday, a plaque was unveiled in his honour at the British Embassy in Berlin. Several of those rescued by Frank travelled there to take part in the ceremony. A statue of Mr Foley now stands outside Highbridge Community Hall. It was put up in his honour in May 2005, on the 47th anniversary of his death, and shows him signing a visa for a Jewish man in a scene that includes the town's clock, bridge and old town hall.

The **first powered flight** took place in Chard in 1848, thanks to the efforts of John Stringfellow (1799–1883), who moved to Chard from Sheffield to work in the lace industry. He had a keen interest in flying machines and worked on the aerial steam carriage, which marked the transition from glider-style flight experiments to powered ones. It was intended to carry passengers, but struggled to fly due to having insufficient power and an engine that was too heavy.

With his friend William Henson, Stringfellow first worked on a design for a model plane with a 20-foot (6-metre) wingspan to be powered by a steam engine. The two friends had dreams of establishing an international company that would make it possible to travel by plane to faraway countries. But although they got as far as building the aircraft, it never flew. When Henson departed for America, Stringfellow continued their work, and built a smaller plane with a wingspan of 10 feet (3 metres), made of a wooden frame covered in silk and powered by a tiny steam engine housed in a gondola below the wings. In a long room in a disused lace mill, in June 1848, Stringfellow successfully flew his plane. His son Fred, who was looking on, wrote: 'The steam was successfully got up after a slight mishap; the machine started down the wire and upon reaching the point of self-detachment, gradually rose until it reached the further end of the room, striking a hole in the canvas placed to stop it.' Stringfellow went on to demonstrate his innovative machine at exhibitions, and paved the way for the likes of the Wright brothers who, just 20 years after Stringfellow's death in 1883, flew the world's first successful manned aircraft.

In a field next to the M5 motorway near Bridgwater stands Somerset's answer to the Angel of the North. The **Willow Man**, or Angel of the South, is an impressive sight at over 40 feet (12 metres) tall, appearing to dance across the fields with arms outstretched and knees bent. He was designed and built in 2000 by sculptor Serena de la Hey, who took four weeks to weave locally grown willow around a metal frame to create the figure, sometimes braving heavy rain and strong winds. The sculpture, commissioned by South West Arts, is intended to celebrate the role of willow in the landscape of the Somerset Levels and Moors, and the tradition of basket-weaving in Somerset.

Willow Man – The Angel of the South!
Creative Commons

Basket making is a treasured Somerset tradition going back to prehistoric times, when willows were woven into wooden trackways in the Brue Valley. The wetlands of Somerset are home to the *Salix triandra*, the ideal willow for weaving, and traditionally every village had its basket makers, who put the Somerset willow to every purpose imaginable. Baskets could be used as fish traps and as boats, when upturned and lined with hide. Wicker furniture was at the height of fashion in the Victorian era. By the end of the nineteenth century, hundreds of people were making their living from growing, selling and weaving the willow, supplying London hotels, the fishing industry and factories in the industrial North.

These tough and versatile baskets played an important role in both world wars, when they were used for transporting pigeons (used as messengers), storing officers' kits, and dropping supplies of ammunition and food to troops. At that time the willow industry was of national importance, and had its own Willow Officer and a research and development programme at the Government Research Station in Bristol. Somerset willow even contributed to the rehabilitation of ex-servicemen who had been blinded by gas: it was policy at the time to teach the blind new skills by which they could earn a living, notably basket making, and so the willow was sent to Institutes for the blind all over the country.

The basket-making industry suffered a decline in the 1950s with the advent of plastics; workshops closed down and hundreds of acres of willows on the Somerset Levels and Moors were 'grubbed out', or cleared of roots and stumps. Today, however, many basket makers are again going strong in the area and still earn a living from their trade. Some 300 to 400 acres of willow are maintained by a dozen families in Somerset, whose skills have been passed down to them through generations.

The 'Cheddar Man' is the **oldest complete human skeleton** ever found in Britain, discovered in 1903 in Gough's Cave at Cheddar Gorge. He was a hunter-gatherer, living in the area about 9,000 years ago, and buried around 1,000 years before the arrival of farming. A sample of DNA was taken from one of Cheddar Man's teeth and compared with that of 20 residents whose families had been living in the area for several generations. Astonishingly, the results revealed a local history teacher to be the living descendant of Cheddar Man, making him the world's most distant confirmed relative!

Cheddar Man reconstruction
Creative Commons

BOOK ENDS

Here are a few more random, but brief, facts about Somerset that warrant a mention, mainly trivia but some are tales!

1. With an area of 1,610 square miles (4,171 sq km) and a population of about 508,000, Somerset is England's seventh-largest county by area but only the 22nd largest by population.

2. The Old English word from which Somerset is derived meant 'people living at or dependent on Somerton'. Although still a thriving market town, Somerton in south Somerset is no longer the county's most important settlement.

3. There are more than 400 villages in Somerset, some of which have wonderful names, such as Beardly Batch, Beer Crocombe, Charlton Mackrell, Chedzoy, Clapton in Gordano, Compton Pauncefoot, Huish Episcopi, Keinton Mandeville, Nempnett Thrubwell, Preston Plucknett and Vobster!

4. Under instructions from the future Emperor Vespasian, the Second Legion Augusta invaded Somerset from the southeast in AD 47. The county remained part of the Roman Empire until around AD 409.

5. Somerset has 11,500 listed buildings, 523 ancient monuments, 192 conservation areas, 41 parks and gardens, 36 English Heritage sites and 19 National Trust sites. Perhaps we can begin to understand why historian Robert Dunning retired from writing the definitive history of the county after 40 years, when he was only halfway through.

6. Other famous sons and daughters of Somerset, not already mentioned in this book, include: Acker Bilk, famous jazz clarinettist; racing driver Jenson Button; recently deceased author Terry Pratchett; Joe Strummer, guitarist and lead singer of the band The Clash; Weston-super-Mare-born Deep Purple and Rainbow guitarist, Ritchie Blackmore; and not forgetting King Arthur, whose 'Camelot' may have been based at Cadbury!

7. King Arthur is also said to be buried in Avalon, the mystical land around Glastonbury, whose abbey is believed to be the oldest 'above-ground' church in the world.

8. According to legend, Joseph of Arimathea, who donated his tomb for the burial of Jesus, came to Britain and asked that the first British church be built near Glastonbury Tor, around 30 years after Jesus's death.

9. Somerset County Cricket Club has made important contributions to English cricket, including the 2005 Ashes hero Marcus Trescothick, and Ian Botham, perhaps the greatest-ever English all-rounder.

10. However, despite this, in 1947 Somerset CCC recorded the lowest ever score by a county cricket club, when they were bowled out for 25 by Gloucestershire!

11. Over 20,000 of the county's population rely on tourism as their only source of income.

ABOVE: King Arthur's possible burial site at Glastonbury Abbey
iStock

LEFT: King Arthur
iStock

12. Seventy-seven per cent of Somerset's population describe themselves as Christians.

13. The town of Shepton Mallet, just south of the Mendip Hills, contains England's oldest civilian prison. It was open from 1610 to 1930, and seven executions took place within its walls between 1889 and 1926.

14. Wells Cathedral is famous for its clock, which was probably in place by 1390. When the clock strikes every quarter, jousting knights rush round above the clock and a Quarter Jack bangs the quarter hours with his heels.

Wells Cathedral
iStock

Wells Cathedral clock
iStock

15. Wells is the smallest city in England, with a population of only 10,536; it's had city status since medieval times because of the presence of Wells Cathedral.

16. In a 1980 episode of Doctor Who, the fourth doctor (played by Tom Baker) says that walking through the Time Vortex 'is a little trick I learnt from a space-time mystic in the Quantocks'.

17. Literary scholars have been unable to agree whether or not Geoffrey Chaucer, author of The Canterbury Tales, took a post as deputy forester at the Royal Forest in North Petherton, on the eastern foothills of the Quantock Hills, in 1391. However, it appears that the forest was administered by the Constable of Windsor, where Chaucer worked as clerk of the works, and it's possible that Chaucer asked the constable for the job because he'd heard the forest was enchanted.

18. Adelard of Bath, a 12th-century Somerset scholar, is credited with having helped to introduce many important mathematical concepts into Western thought, including the Arabic idea of 'zero'.

19. Somerset has two gorges: as well as the most well-known Cheddar Gorge there's also Ebbor Gorge, which contains two geologically important caves that hold the bones of Ice Age mammals.

20. Taunton was the first town in the country to be lit permanently by electric street lighting in 1881.

21. The West Somerset Railway, opened in 1862, is the longest preserved steam railway in the country at 22.75 miles (36.61km).

West Somerset Railway — Creative Commons Geof Sheppard

22.Nunney Castle is a perfect gem of a moated castle and the only one of its type in England.

23.Hestercombe Gardens is a unique collection of three gardens spanning three centuries of garden history and design: Coplestone Warre Bampfylde's Georgian landscape garden; the Victorian terrace and shrubbery; and the stunning Edwardian garden design by Sir Edwin Lutyens and Gertrude Jekyll.

24.The church at Oare was the setting for many scenes from Lorna Doone, a novel by Richard Blackmore. His grandfather was the vicar here and Blackmore's visits as a boy had a powerful effect. Lorna Doone is married in the church and Carver Doone fires the shot that spills Lorna's blood on the altar steps.

25.Colonel John Chard won the Victoria Cross for his part in the defence of Rorke's Drift when it was attacked by Zulus in January 1879. John died at Hatch Beauchamp, near Taunton, in 1897.

26. The purebred Exmoor Pony has inhabited the Exmoor moorland since ancient times and is the oldest breed of pony in Britain.

Exmoor ponies in the Valley of Rocks — Creative Commons

27. Over 400 different varieties of cider apple are grown in Somerset.

28. Wellow, near Bath, is the birthplace of John Bull (1562–1628), organist of the Chapel Royal and the man who is believed to have written the music for the National Anthem.

29. St Beuno's Church at Culbone, hidden away in a secluded dell by the sea and only reachable on foot, not far from Porlock, is the smallest church in England, at just 35 feet (10.5m) by 12 feet (3.7m).

St Beuno's Church, Culbone
Creative Commons Richard Mascall

30. The Manor House at Cricket St Thomas, near Chard, was used as the setting for the TV series To the Manor Born, starring Penelope Keith. It's now a hotel.

Other books in the Bradwell Books Tales & Trivia series

Available Now

Dorset Tales & Trivia

Wiltshire Tales & Trivia

Hampshire Tales & Trivia

Other titles for these counties include

Hampshire

Hampshire Dialect

Bradwell's Eclectica Hampshire

Bradwell's Eclectica Southampton

Hampshire Ghost Stories

Hampshire Wit & Humour

Walks for all Ages Hampshire *out in 2016*

Legends & Folklore Hampshire *out 2016*

Dorset

Walks for all Ages Dorset

Dorset Ghost Stories

Dorset Wit & Humour

Dorset Dialect

Legends & Folklore Dorset *out 2016*

Wiltshire

Wiltshire Dialect

Wiltshire Ghost Stories

Wiltshire Legends & Folklore

Walks for all Ages Wiltshire

Wiltshire Wit & Humour

Somerset

Somerset Dialect

Somerset Ghost Stories

Somerset Wit & Humour

Walks for all Ages Somerset

Walks for all Ages Exmoor

Legends & Folklore Somerset *out 2016*

For more details of these books
and other books you may be
interested in, visit
www.bradwellbooks.com

BIBLIOGRAPHY

A History of Somerset, Robert Dunning, Phillimore, 1983

Somerset Curiosities, Enid Byford, Dovecote Press Paperbacks, 1987

I Never Knew That About England, Christopher Winn, Random House Group, 2008

The Rough Guide to Bath, Bristol and Somerset,
Rough Guides, 2012

Websites accessed February–April 2015

en.wikipedia.org/wiki/Minehead#May_Day_Hobby_Horse

www.bbc.co.uk/news/uk-england-29742774

www.visitsomerset.co.uk/whats-on/carnivals

en.wikipedia.org/wiki/West_Country_Carnival

www.bridgwatercarnival.org.uk/useful-info/squibbing/

www.bbc.co.uk/somerset/content/articles/2005/01/21/somerset_
celebrities_a_to_h_feature.shtml

www.somersetcountygazette.co.uk/news/taunton_news/10962819.Top_10_
celebrity_links_to_Taunton/?ref=rss

www.westerndailypress.co.uk/Somerset-s-oldest-traditions/story-12301855-
detail/story.html

en.wikipedia.org/wiki/Wassailing#The_Orchard-visiting_Wassail

www.kevanmanwaring.co.uk/bookofthebardicchair.html

www.bbc.co.uk/news/uk-england-somerset-30687171

www.independent.co.uk/news/uk/home-news/the-somerset-village-
thats-having-to-put-a-stop-to-more-than-100-fairy-doors-appearing-in-the-
woods-10086135.html

www.independent.co.uk/news/uk/this-britain/around-a-county-in-40-
facts-a-very-brief-history-of-somerset-462828.html

www.independent.co.uk/news/uk/this-britain/around-a-county-in-40-facts-a-very-brief-history-of-somerset-462828.html

www.somersetguardian.co.uk/Oldest-skittles-league-country-celebrates-80/story-19123042-detail/story.html

www.somersetmade.co.uk/oldscrump/history-cider.php

innorthsomerset.co.uk/case-studies/thatchers-sandford

www.andreazuvich.com/history/taunton-castle-the-bloody-assizes/

en.wikipedia.org/wiki/Monmouth_Rebellion

www.haunted-britain.com/taunton-castle.htm

www.baldhiker.com/2011/07/18/wells-somerset-a-little-city-with-a-big-history/

www.britainexpress.com/Where_to_go_in_Britain/Destination_Library/wells.htm www.crownatwells.co.uk/hot-fuzz.html

www.cheddarvillage.org.uk/cheddar-cheese/

www.cheddargorgecheeseco.co.uk/acatalog/about-cheddar-gorge.html

www.bubblegun.com/features/cleese.html

en.wikipedia.org/wiki/John_Cleese

www.northsomersettimes.co.uk/what-s-on/john_cleese_at_the_colston_hall_1_3715272

news.bbc.co.uk/local/bristol/hi/people_and_places/newsid_8920000/8920365.stm

www.cheddarvalleygazette.co.uk/Lord-Rinds-honeymoon-Cheddar-Gorge-inspired-JRR/story-26229127-detail/story.html

www.westerndailypress.co.uk/MAN-MYTH/story-12335757-detail/story.html

www.telegraph.co.uk/gardening/3302297/Literary-landscape-Coleridges-Somerset.html

www.visit-exmoor.co.uk/coleridge-way/coleridge-way-home-page

en.wikipedia.org/wiki/Bath_Somerset

en.wikipedia.org/wiki/Wookey_Hole_Caves

en.wikipedia.org/wiki/Glastonbury_Festival

www.mirror.co.uk/news/uk-news/glastonbury-2014-numbers-facts-figures-3741860

en.wikipedia.org/wiki/Chalice_Well

en.wikipedia.org/wiki/Beast_of_Exmoor

www.greekmythology.com/Olympians/Hermes/hermes.html

www.independent.co.uk/news/uk/this-britain/around-a-county-in-40-facts-a-very-brief-history-of-somerset-462828.html

www.westerndailypress.co.uk/East-Coker-graveyard-reunite-TS-Eliot-widow/story-17565928-detail/story.html

en.wikipedia.org/wiki/Four_Quartets

www.theguardian.com/artanddesign/2014/oct/24/beatles-minehead-train-marian-keery-cynthia-wilkinson

westsomersetrailway.vticket.co.uk/article.php/771/beatles-film-night-a-hard-days-night

www.somersetcountygazette.co.uk/news/9963586.Previously_unseen_shots_of_The_Beatles_in_a_Taunton_chippy/

en.wikipedia.org/wiki/Adge_Cutler

www.theimportanceofbeingtrivial.com/where-jack-and-jill-really-did-go-up-the-hill.html

www.telegraph.co.uk/travel/719832/UK-Somerset-plays-a-Romantic-lead.html

www.biography.com/people/haile-selassie-i-9325096#early-years

www.bbc.co.uk/guides/zqqx6sg

en.wikipedia.org/wiki/Haile_Selassie

www.houseofhismajesty.com/tag/rastafari/

hmd.org.uk/resources/stories/frank-foley-0

www.burnham-on-sea.com/frank-foley.shtml

en.wikipedia.org/wiki/History_of_Somerset

en.wikipedia.org/wiki/Sweet_Track

Kevin
Mayhew

We hope you enjoy the music in this book.
Further copies are available from your local
music shop or Christian bookshop.

In case of difficulty, please contact the publisher direct by writing to:

The Sales Department
KEVIN MAYHEW LTD
Rattlesden
Bury St Edmunds
Suffolk IP30 0SZ

Please ask for our complete catalogue of outstanding Church Music.

First published in 1997 in Great Britain by Kevin Mayhew Ltd.

© Copyright 1997 Kevin Mayhew Ltd.

ISBN 0 86209 987 0
ISMN M 57004 045 2
Catalogue No: 1450071

0 1 2 3 4 5 6 7 8 9

Front cover illustration by Darren Regan
Cover designed by Jaquetta Sergeant

Music Editor: Nicola Greengrass
Music setting by Tracy Cracknell

Printed and bound in Great Britain

Contents

1 The world is full of smelly feet

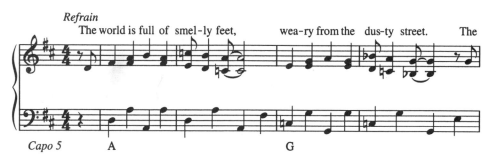

2. People on a dusty journey
   need a place to rest;
   Jesus says, 'You say you love me,
   this will be the test!'

3. We're his friends, we recognise him
   in the folk we meet;
   smart or scruffy, we'll still love him,
   wash his smelly feet!

Words: Michael Forster
Music: Christopher Tambling

2 Love is like a circle

Jauntily

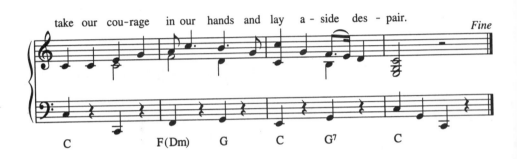

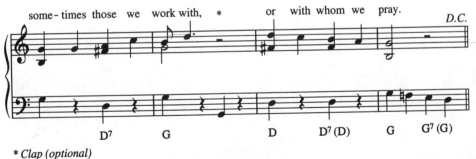

* *Clap (optional)*

2. Sometimes it's a granny,
   mother or a dad,
   sometimes it's a baby,
   smiling or so sad.

3. Love can come from adults
   and from girls and boys;
   love can come in silence
   or within the noise.

4. Some find love through list'ning,
   some through ardent prayer,
   others in the scriptures,
   some through tender care.

5. Love can make us happy,
   love can bring us tears,
   love can make us peaceful,
   casting out our fears

Last refrain:
   But in all our loving,
   from beginning to the end,
   the love we share all comes from God
   who greets us in each friend.

Words: W.L. Wallace
Music: Martin Setchell

3 There was one, there were two
The children's band

2. Drums are going to boom in praise of Jesus,
   praise of Jesus, praise of Jesus,
   drums are going to boom in praise of Jesus,
   praising Jesus the Lord.

3. Tambourines will shake in praise of Jesus,
   praise of Jesus, praise of Jesus,
   tambourines will shake in praise of Jesus,
   praising Jesus the Lord.

4. Trumpets will resound in praise of Jesus,
   praise of Jesus, praise of Jesus,
   trumpets will resound in praise of Jesus,
   praising Jesus the Lord.

Verses may be added ad lib, for example:

Clarinets will swing in praise of Jesus . . .

Play recorders, too . . .

Triangles will ting . . .

Fiddles will be scraped . . .

Let guitars be strummed . . .

Chime bars will be chimed . . .

Glockenspiels will play . . .

Vibraphones will throb . . .

Trombones slide about . . .

Words: Christina Wilde
Music: traditional American melody, arr. Noel Rawsthorne

4 Stand up! Walk tall

Refrain
Stand up! Walk tall in the house of God! Stand up! Walk tall in the

G   Am   D[7]

house of God! Stand up! Walk tall in the house of God and

G   C   G   Am

say that we be-long! *Fine* 1. It makes no diff-'rence who we are,

G D[7] G   Am   D[7]

or what we may have done; it

G   Am   B[7]   Em

does-n't mat-ter where we're from, for

Am   D⁷   G

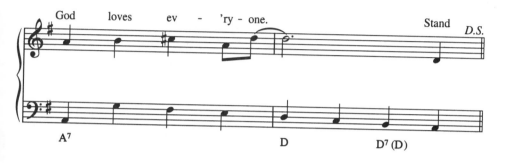

God loves ev - 'ry - one.   Stand   D.S.

A⁷   D   D⁷ (D)

2. Whatever people think or say,
   we need not be afraid.
   We're members of the human race,
   the people God has made.

3. So, male or female, black or white,
   of any age or race,
   we're not afraid to stand up straight
   and look God in the face!

Words: Michael Forster
Music: Christopher Tambling

5 Stand on the corner of the street
God is living everywhere

Cheerfully
Refrain

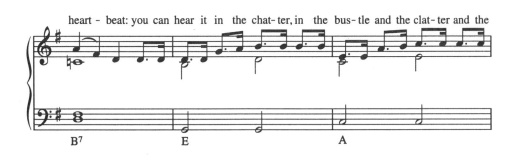

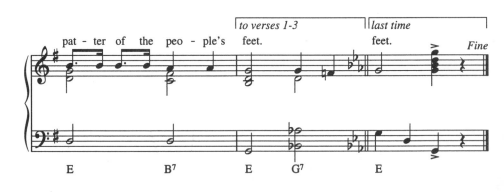

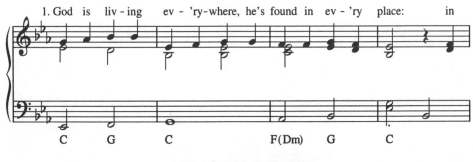

crowd- ed squares and shop- ping streets you'll al-ways see his face.

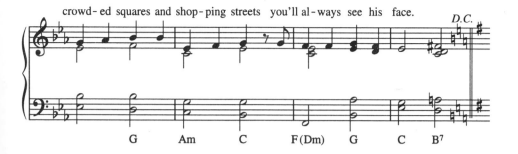

G   Am   C   F (Dm)   G   C   B⁷

2. God is living ev'rywhere
   that human life is found.
   In cafés, shops and car parks, too,
   his Spirit is around.

3. God is living ev'rywhere,
   in all the human race,
   in schools and flats and offices,
   in ev'rybody's face.

Words: Richard Farrow
Music: Andrew Gant

6 I'm glad I'm alive

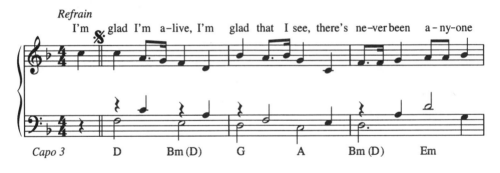

loves my fing - ers, God loves my tum-my and my nose. I'm

D.S.

F♯(C♯dim⁷) Bm (D)　　G　　　A　　　D　G(–)　D　A⁷(–)

2. I love my lips, yes, I love my teeth,
   I love my legs and my toes.
   I love my arms, I love my fingers,
   I love my tummy and my nose.

Words: W.L. Wallace
Music: Richard Lloyd

7 God sends a rainbow
Colours of hope

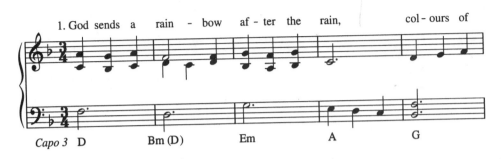

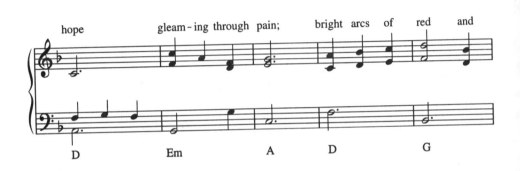

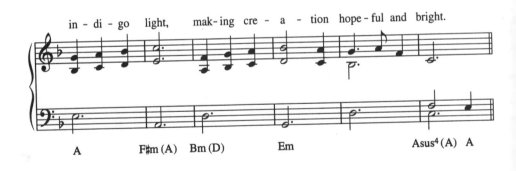

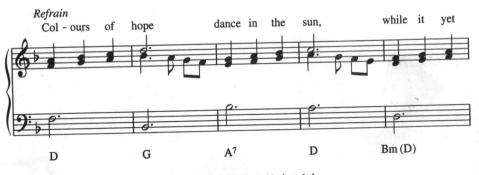

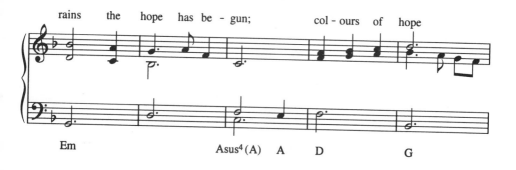

rains the hope has be - gun; col - ours of hope

Em   Asus⁴(A)   A   D   G

shine through the rain,   col - ours of love,   noth - ing is vain.

A⁷   D   Bm (D)   G   Asus⁴(A) A⁷(A) D

2. When we are lonely, when we're afraid,
   though it seems dark, rainbows are made;
   even when life itself has to end,
   God is our rainbow, God is our friend.

3. Where people suffer pain or despair,
   God can be seen in those who care;
   even where war and hatred abound,
   rainbows of hope are still to be found.

4. People themselves like rainbows are made,
   colours of hope in us displayed;
   old ones and young ones, women and men,
   all can be part of love's great 'Amen'!

Words: Michael Forster
Music: Christopher Tambling

8 Sing praise to God

With a swing

Capo 5

1. Sing praise to God, sing praise to God for life, for

beau-ty, hope and love, for ten-der-ness and grace.

Sing praise to God, sing praise to God for life,

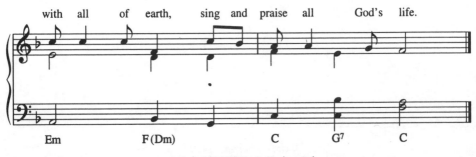

with all of earth, sing and praise all God's life.

2. Lift up your eyes to see the works of God,
   in ev'ry blade of grass, in ev'ry human face.
   Lift up your eyes to see the works of God,
   through all of life, in all time and all space.

3. Open your ears to hear the cries of pain
   arising from the poor and all who are oppressed.
   Open your mind and use your wits to find
   who are the cause of this world's unjust ways.

4. Reach out your hands to share the wealth God gave
   with those who are oppressed, and those who feel alone.
   Reach out your hands and gently touch with Christ
   each frozen heart which has said 'No' to love.

5. Open our hearts to love the world with Christ,
   each person in this world, each creature of this earth.
   Open our hearts to love the ones who hate,
   and in their hearts find a part of ourself.

6. Live life with love, for love encircles all;
   it casts out all our fears, it fills the heart with joy.
   Live life with love, for love transforms our life,
   as we praise God with our eyes, hands and hearts.

Words: W.L. Wallace
Music: Noel Rawsthorne

9 God was born on earth
Never mind the sheep, look for the baby

Allegretto

1. God was born on earth, a

Capo 3   D   A⁷

home - less stran - ger, fac - ing ev - 'ry kind of mor - tal dan - ger,

D   Em   B⁷   Em   A

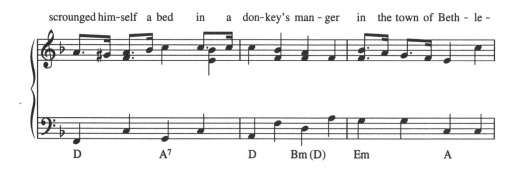

scrounged him-self a bed in a don-key's man - ger in the town of Beth - le -

D   A⁷   D   Bm (D)   Em   A

hem.   *Refrain*   Ne - ver mind the sheep, look for the ba - by,

D   A   Dm   A   F (Dm)   Dm

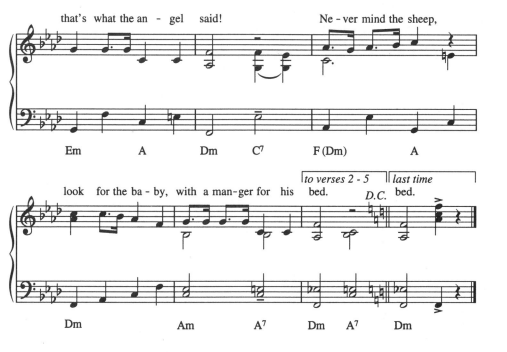

that's what the an - gel said! Ne - ver mind the sheep, look for the ba - by, with a man-ger for his bed.

2. Shepherds in the fields with sheep to care for,
   angels said, 'What are you sitting there for?
   Never mind the questions, the whys and wherefores,
   get along to Bethlehem!'

3. 'Never mind the sheep, look for the baby,
   he's the one to watch, I don't mean maybe.
   If you want to share in this special day, be
   sure to go to Bethlehem.'

4. So they left the sheep and went out looking,
   eager to find out what God had cooking,
   found a classic problem of overbooking
   in the town of Bethlehem.

5. Jesus doesn't put on airs and graces,
   Likes to be in unexpected places,
   comes to us in smiles and warm embraces,
   as he did at Bethlehem.

Words: Michael Forster
Music: Andrew Gant

10 Hee, haw! Hee, haw!
The donkey's Christmas carol

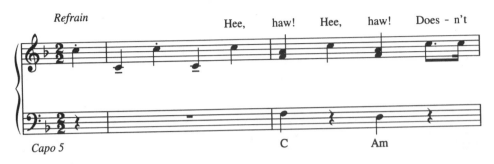

2. After all that journey,
   with my heavy load,
   did I ever once complain about the dreadful road?
   I can cope with backache,
   and these swollen feet.
   All I ask is some respect, and one square meal to eat.

3. 'Be prepared,' I told them,
   'better book ahead.'
   Joseph said, 'Don't be an ass,' and took a chance instead.
   Now they've pinched my bedroom,
   people are so rude!
   I can cope with that, but not a baby in my food!

Words: Michael Forster
Music: Noel Rawsthorne

11 God turned darkness into light

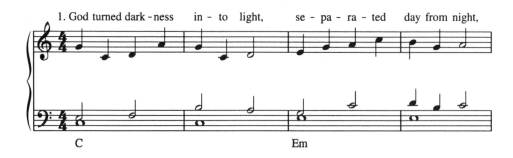

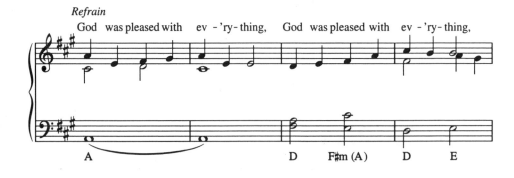

2. God divided land and sea,
   filled the world with plants and trees,
   all so beautiful to see,
   and declared that it was good.

3. God made animals galore,
   fishes, birds and dinosaurs,
   heard the splashes, songs and roars,
   and declared that it was good.

4. God made people last of all,
   black and white, and short and tall,
   male and female, large and small,
   and declared that it was good.

Words: Michael Forster
Music: Christopher Tambling

12 We thank God for the harvest
Gotta get out and scatter some seed

With a swing

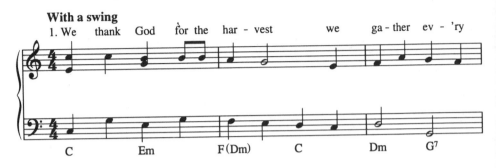

1. We thank God for the har - vest we ga - ther ev - 'ry

C   Em   F(Dm)   C   Dm   G7

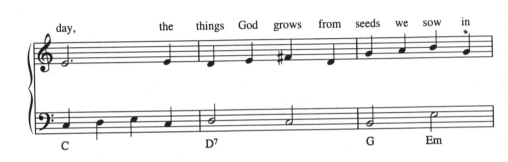

day,   the things God grows from seeds we sow in

C   D7   G   Em

all our work and play.   *Refrain*   Got - ta get out and scat - ter some

Am   D7   G   C

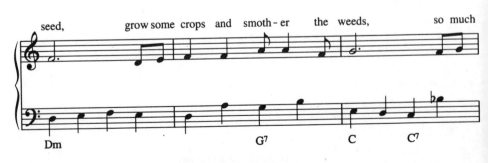

seed,   grow some crops and smoth - er the weeds,   so much

Dm   G7   C   C7

love there's no room for greed, got-ta go and scat-ter some seeds.

F (Dm)　　　　　　G　　C　　G⁷　　　　　C

2. God gives love to be scattered,
   and seeds of faith to sow,
   then sprinkles grace in ev'ry place
   to make the harvest grow.

3. We can work all together,
   with people ev'rywhere:
   in ev'ry place, each creed and race,
   God gives us love to share.

Words: Christine Wilde
Music: Noel Rawsthorne

13 I am cold, I am ice

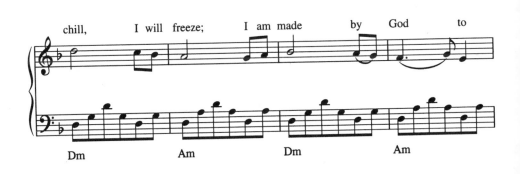

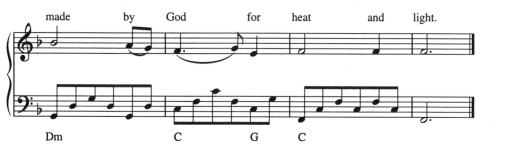

made by God for heat and light.

Dm   C   G   C

2. I am frost, I am snow,
   I will sparkle and shine;
   I am made by God
   to clean the earth.

3. I am rain, I am hail,
   I will drive, I will splash;
   I am made by God
   to feed the earth.

4. I am air, I am wind,
   I will move, I will blow;
   I am made by God
   to clean the sky.

5. I am sun, I am fire,
   I will warm with my flames;
   I am made by God
   for heat and light.

Words: W.L. Wallace
Music: James Patten

14 There's a great big world out there

2. We've brought to God our prayers and hymns,
   now it's time to live his life,
   to sow a little love and peace
   in the place of selfish strife.

3. We've listened to the word of God,
   now it's time to live it out,
   to show by ev'rything we do
   what the gospel is about.

This may be sung as a round during the third verse with the second voices entering at
the refrain (using the accompaniment to the verse).

Words: Michael Forster
Music: Andrew Gant

15 Jesus calls us to a party
Just a little bit of bread and a little bit of wine

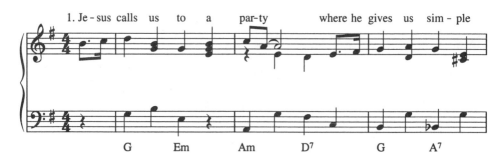

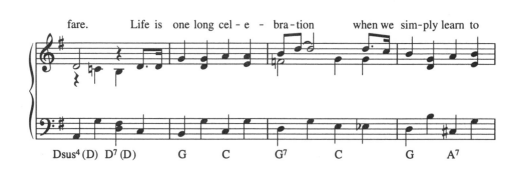

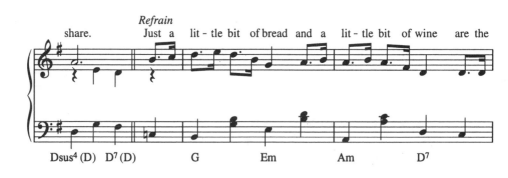

lit – tle bit of wine,   and we've got   a   feast   in – deed!

Am   D⁷   G   A⁷(–) D⁷   G

2. We don't need a fancy menu,
   just the basic things will do;
   Jesus gives us love for sharing
   and he says to me and you:

3. Jesus gave himself for others
   when he died to set us free.
   Now he leads the celebration,
   he's alive in you and me!

Words: Michael Forster
Music: Christopher Tambling

16 We eat the plants that grow from the seed

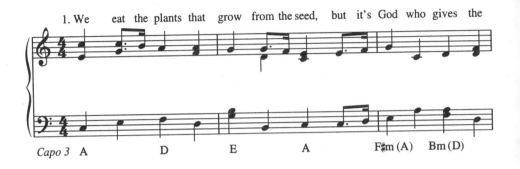

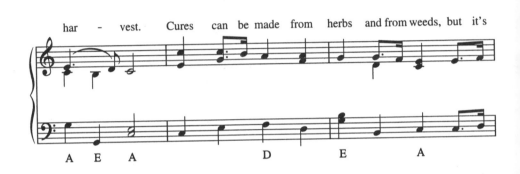

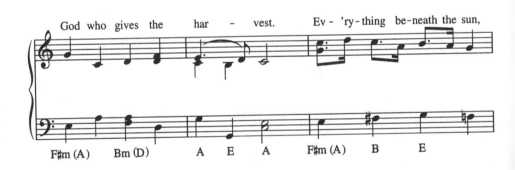

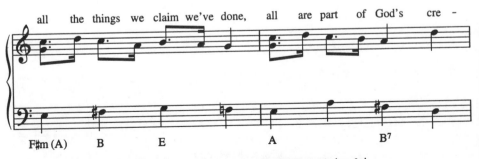

a – tion: we can meet peo - ple's needs with

E A D

things we grow from seed, but it's God who gives the har - vest.

E A Bm (D) E A

2. We find the iron and turn it to steel,
   but it's God who gives the harvest.
   We pull the levers, we turn the wheels,
   but it's God who gives the harvest.
   Ev'rything we say we've made,
   plastic bags to metal spades,
   all are part of God's creation:
   we can make lots of things
   from microchips to springs,
   but it's God who gives the harvest.

Words: Susan Mee
Music: traditional English melody, arr. Noel Rawsthorne

17 Praise God in his holy place

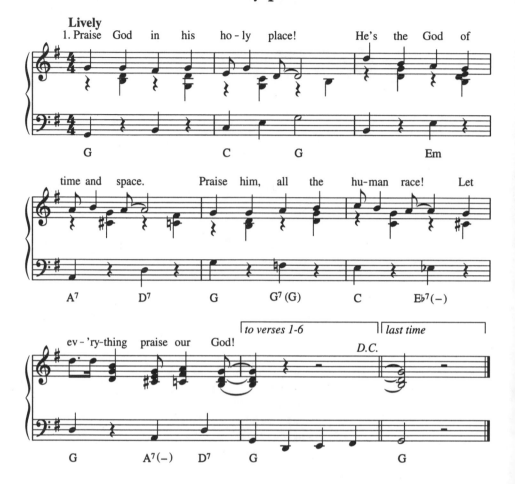

2. Praise him with the ol' wood block!
   Let it swing and let it rock,
   praising God around the clock!
   Let ev'rything praise our God!

3. Praise him with the big bass drum,
   if you've got guitars, then strum!
   Now let's make those rafters hum!
   Let ev'rything praise our God!

4. Praise him with the chime bars' chime,
   tell the bells it's party time,
   help those singers find a rhyme!
   Let ev'rything praise our God!

5. Violin or xylophone,
   trumpets with their awesome tone;
   bowed or beaten, bashed or blown,
   let ev'rything praise our God!

6. Cymbals, triangles and things,
   if it crashes, howls or rings,
   ev'rybody shout and sing!
   Let ev'rything praise our God!

Words: Michael Forster
Music: Christopher Tambling

18 Each of us is a living stone

Living stones

Brightly (swinging)

Refrain

Each of us is a liv-ing stone no one needs to stand a - lone,

Capo 3   D   A⁷   D

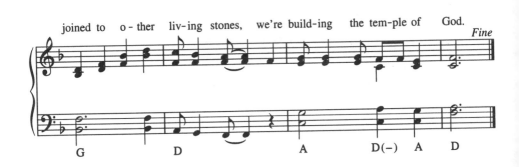

joined to o - ther liv-ing stones, we're build-ing the tem-ple of God.

Fine

G   D   A   D(–)   A   D

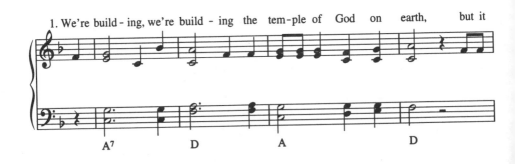

1. We're build - ing, we're build - ing the tem-ple of God on earth, but it

A⁷   D   A   D

needs no walls or stee - ple, for we're ma - king a house of grea - ter worth, we're

A⁷   D   A⁷   D

build - ing it with peo - ple!

D.C.

G D A⁷ D A A⁷

2. The stone that, the stone that the builders once cast aside
   has been made the firm foundation,
   and the carpenter who was crucified
   now offers us salvation.

Words: Michael Forster
Music: James Patten

19 God has spoken

Bright and rhythmic

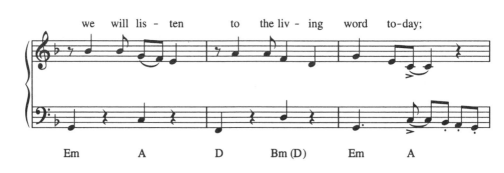

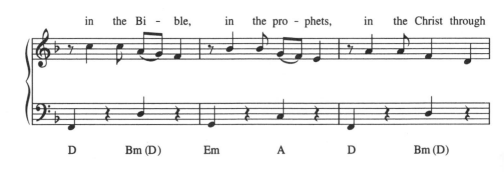

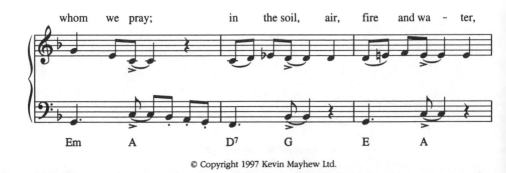

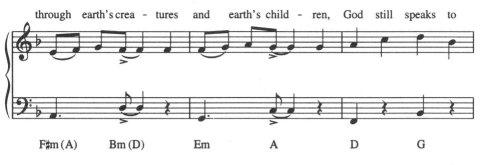

through earth's crea - tures   and   earth's child - ren,   God   still   speaks   to

F#m (A)   Bm (D)   Em   A   D   G

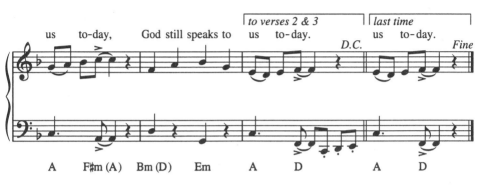

to verses 2 & 3 | *last time*

us   to-day,   God still speaks to   us   to-day.   us   to- day.

D.C.   Fine

A   F#m (A) Bm (D)   Em   A   D   A   D

2. God has spoken, we will listen
   to the living word today;
   in the lovers, in the dreamers,
   in what fearless critics say;
   through the writers, actors, dancers,
   poets, artists, clowns and weavers,
   God still speaks to us today,
   God still speaks to us today.

3. God has spoken, we will listen
   to the living word today;
   through the media, in the text books,
   through our study, work and play;
   on computers, 'phones and faxes,
   through our senses, humour, wisdom,
   God still speaks to us today,
   God still speaks to us today.

Words: W.L. Wallace
Music: Martin Setchell

20 Jesus went away to the desert
Ain't listenin' to no temptation

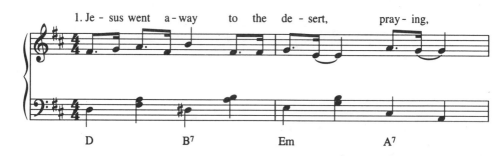

1. Je - sus went a - way to the de - sert, pray - ing,

D   B7   Em   A7

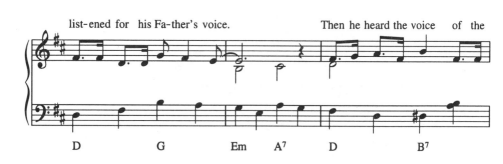

list-ened for his Fa-ther's voice.   Then he heard the voice of the

D   G   Em   A7   D   B7

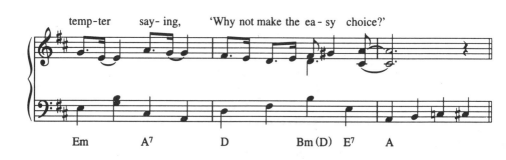

temp-ter say- ing,   'Why not make the ea - sy choice?'

Em   A7   D   Bm (D) E7   A

Refrain

Ain't lis - t'nin' to   no temp - ta - tion,   ain't fall - in' for

D   F (Dm)

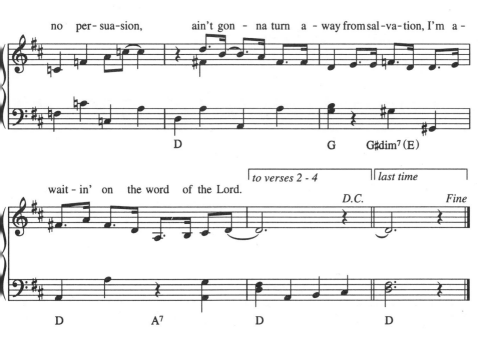

no per-sua-sion, ain't gon - na turn a - way from sal-va-tion, I'm a-wait - in' on the word of the Lord.

D

G   G#dim⁷ (E)

to verses 2 - 4   *last time*

D.C.   *Fine*

D   A⁷   D   D

2. 'There's an easy way if you'd only choose it,
   you can turn the stones to bread!
   What's the good of pow'r if you don't abuse it?
   Gotta keep yourself well fed!'

3. 'What about a stunt to attract attention,
   showing off your special pow'r?
   You'd get more applause than I'd care to mention
   jumping from the Temple tow'r!'

4. 'Ev'rything you want will be right there for you,
   listen to the words I say!
   Nobody who matters will dare ignore you;
   my way is the easy way.'

Words: Michael Forster
Music: Christopher Tambling

21 Everyone's a Christmas baby

With a swing

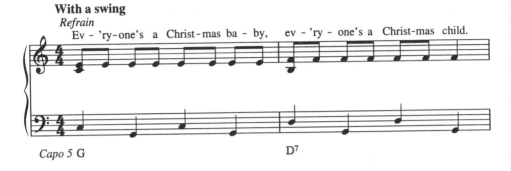

God is smil-ing up at us from ev-'ry girl and boy. Yes!

D.C.

D⁷   G   E   Am   D⁷   G

2. Christmas comes on ev'ry day,
   and in ev'ry kind of place,
   for each new child that's born on earth
   reveals God's love and grace. Yes!

3. Life and hope begin anew
   when another child is born,
   and ev'ry morning that we awake
   is like a new world's dawn. Yes!

Words: Sarah Forth
Music: Noel Rawsthorne

22 God is the centre and the circle

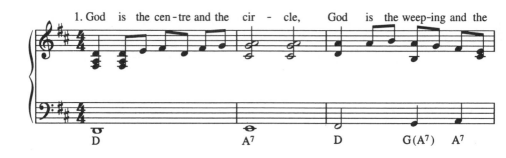

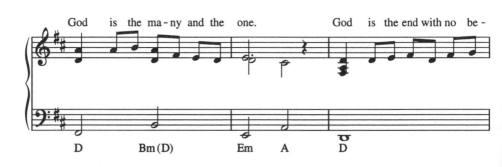

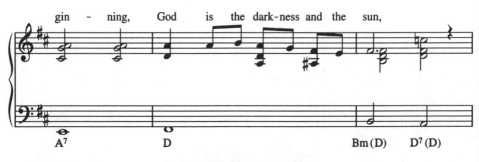

God is the death and God the liv - ing, God is the ma-ny and the one.

G   Em   D   A⁷   D

2. God is the binding and the freedom,
   God is aloneness and embrace,
   God is the peace and God the struggle,
   God is the nameless and the face.
   God is the centre and the circle,
   God is the weeping and the fun,
   God is the dancing and the stillness,
   God is the many and the one.

Words: W.L. Wallace
Music: Andrew Gant

23 Do you ever wish you could fly
Just be glad God made you 'you'

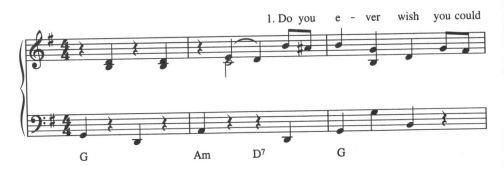

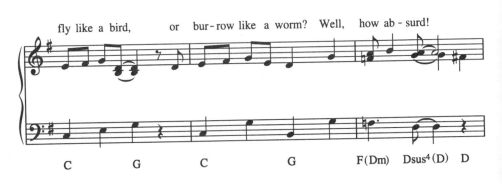

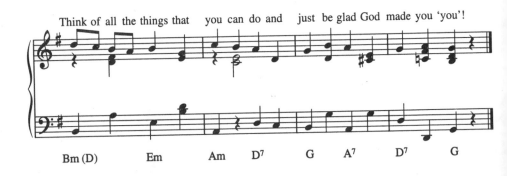

2. Do you ever wish you could swim like a duck?
   Unless your feet are webbed you're out of luck!
   Think of all the things that you can do
   and just be glad God made you 'you'!

3. Do you ever wish you could run like a hare?
   Well, wishing it won't get you anywhere!
   Think of all the things that you can do
   and just be glad God made you 'you'!

4. Do you ever wish you could hang like a bat?
   There's really not a lot of fun in that!
   Think of all the things that you can do
   and just be glad God made you 'you'!

5. Do you ever wish – well, that's really enough!
   To wish away your life is silly stuff!
   Think of all the things that you can do
   and just be glad God made you 'you'!

Words: Michael Forster
Music: Christopher Tambling

24 There are people who live in mansions
Gotta put the world to rights

2. There are people who feed on salmon,
there are people who feed on stew,
there are people who hardly feed at all,
and God says that won't do!

3. There are people with famous faces,
there are people with famous names,
there are people whom no one knows at all,
and God says that's a shame.

Words: Dave Davidson
Music: Noel Rawsthorne

25 We are one family together

Gently

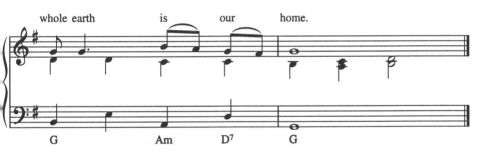

2. We care for creatures and for plant life,
   we care for ev'rything that lives.
   We care for soil, for air and water,
   the whole earth is our home.

3. We care for children and for adults,
   we care for those who are oppressed.
   We care for justice and for sharing,
   the whole earth is our home.

4. We are one family together,
   we are one family in God.
   We are one family together,
   the whole earth is our home.

Words: W.L. Wallace
Music: Norman Warren

Index of Uses / Scriptural References